AMERICA:
THE QUIZ

AMERICA:
THE QUIZ

HOW WELL DO YOU KNOW
YOUR COUNTRY?

FALL RIVER PRESS

New York

FALL RIVER PRESS

New York

An Imprint of Sterling Publishing
1166 Avenue of the Americas
New York, NY 10036

Jacket design by Elizabeth Lindy

ISBN 978-1-4351-6021-7

For information about custom editions, special sales, and
premium and corporate purchases, please contact Sterling Special Sales at
800-805-5489 or specialsales@sterlingpublishing.com.

Manufactured in the United States of America

2 4 6 8 10 9 7 5 3 1

www.sterlingpublishing.com

Contents

Introduction

Becoming an American citizen is a rite of passage that millions of people have undertaken during the country's existence. During the nineteenth and early twentieth centuries, citizenship tests were usually administered orally by judges in courtrooms. Starting in 1906, the federal Bureau of Naturalization began to standardize and federalize a process that up until then had been handled by the courts at the local level in ways that varied widely from one jurisdiction to the next.

The Bureau also began a program to educate prospective citizens about the United States' civics and history. As a result of that process, the United States Citizenship and Immigration Department now provides a list of 100 questions that must be studied by all citizenship applicants for the civics portion of the test. A United States Citizenship and Immigration Services (USCIS) officer asks the applicant ten questions from that list. The applicant must answer six questions correctly in order to pass.

Between October 1, 2009 and August 31, 2014, USCIS officers administered nearly 3.7 million tests. The overall pass rate for the civics and English tests was 91 percent as of August 2014. According to *USA Today*, in 2012 the applicant pass rate for the civics test was 93 percent. However, a telephone poll by the Center for the Study of the American Dream at Xavier University in Cincinnati revealed that just 65 percent of native-born Americans were able to provide six out of ten correct answers to questions from the same test.

How many questions do you think you will be able to answer correctly? Take the test to find out!

American Government

I n the United States, the government gets its power to govern from the people. We have a government of the people, by the people, and for the people. Citizens in the United States shape their government and its policies, so they must learn about important public issues and get involved in their communities. Learning about American government helps you understand your rights and responsibilities and allows you to fully participate in the American political process. The Founders of this country decided that the United States should be a representative democracy. They wanted a nation ruled by laws, not by men. In a representative democracy, the people choose officials to make laws and represent their views and concerns in government. The following section will help you understand the principles of American democracy, the U.S. system of government, and the important rights and responsibilities of U.S. citizenship.

PRINCIPLES
of AMERICAN
DEMOCRACY

Question 1

What is the supreme law of the land?

Handwritten note at top: 3 MAY / 1791 → Polish Constitution (first in Europe)

Answer 1

• The Constitution

The Founding Fathers of the United States wrote the Constitution in 1787. The Constitution is the "supreme law of the land." The U.S. Constitution has lasted longer than any other country's constitution. It establishes the basic principles of the United States government. The Constitution establishes a system of government called "representative democracy." In a representative democracy, citizens choose representatives to make the laws. U.S. citizens also choose a president to lead the executive branch of government. The Constitution lists fundamental rights for all citizens and other people living in the United States. Laws made in the United States must follow the Constitution.

Question 2

What does the Constitution do?

Answer 2

- **sets up the government**
- **defines the government**
- **protects basic rights of Americans**

The Constitution of the United States divides government power between the national government and state governments. The name for this division of power is "federalism." Federalism is an important idea in the Constitution. We call the Founding Fathers who wrote the Constitution the "Framers" of the Constitution. The Framers wanted to limit the powers of the government, so they separated the powers into three branches: executive, legislative, and judicial. The Constitution explains the power of each branch. The Constitution also includes changes and additions, called "amendments." The first ten amendments are called the "Bill of Rights." The Bill of Rights established the individual rights and liberties of all Americans.

Question 3

The idea of self-government is in the first three words of the Constitution. What are these words?

Answer 3

• We the People

The Constitution says:

> *We the People of the United States, in Order to form a more perfect Union, establish Justice, insure domestic Tranquility, provide for the common defence, promote the general Welfare, and secure the Blessings of Liberty to ourselves and our Posterity, do ordain and establish this Constitution for the United States of America.*

With the words "We the People," the Constitution states that the people set up the government. The government works for the people and protects the rights of people. In the United States, the power to govern comes from the people, who are the highest power. This is called "popular sovereignty." The people elect representatives to make laws.

Question 4

What is an amendment?

Answer 4

- a change (to the Constitution)
- an addition (to the Constitution)

An amendment is a change or addition to the Constitution.
The Framers of the Constitution knew that laws can change
as a country grows. They did not want to make it too easy
to modify the Constitution, the supreme law of the land.
The Framers also did not want the Constitution to lose
its meaning. For this reason, the Framers decided that
Congress could pass amendments in only two ways: by
a two-thirds vote in the U.S. Senate and the House of
Representatives or by a special convention. A special
convention has to be requested by two-thirds of the
states. After an amendment has passed in Congress or
by a special convention, the amendment must then be
ratified (accepted) by the legislatures of three-fourths
of the states. The amendment can also be ratified by a
special convention in three-fourths of the states. Not
all proposed amendments are ratified. Six times in U.S.
history amendments have passed in Congress but were
not approved by enough states to be ratified.

Question 5

What do we call the first ten amendments to the Constitution?

Answer 5

• the Bill of Rights

The Bill of Rights is the first ten amendments to the
Constitution. When the Framers wrote the Constitution,
they did not focus on individual rights. They focused
on creating the system and structure of government.
Many Americans believed that the Constitution should
guarantee the rights of the people, and they wanted a
list of all the things a government could not do. They
were afraid that a strong government would take away
the rights people won in the Revolutionary War. James
Madison, one of the Framers of the Constitution, wrote
a list of individual rights and limits on the government.
These rights are the first ten amendments. Some of these
rights include freedom of expression, the right to bear
arms, freedom from search without warrant, freedom not
to be tried twice for the same crime, the right to not testify
against yourself, the right to a trial by a jury of your peers,
the right to an attorney, and protection against excessive
fines and unusual punishments. The Bill of Rights was
ratified in 1791.

Question 6

What is one right or freedom from the First Amendment?

Answer 6

- **speech**
- **religion**
- **assembly**
- **press**
- **petition the government**

The First Amendment of the Bill of Rights protects a person's right to freedom of expression. Freedom of expression allows open discussion and debate on public issues. Open discussion and debate are important to democracy. The First Amendment also protects freedom of religion and free speech. This amendment says that Congress may not pass laws that establish an official religion and may not limit religious expression. Congress may not pass laws that limit freedom of the press or the right of people to meet peacefully. The First Amendment also gives people the right to petition the government to change laws or acts that are not fair. Congress may not take away these rights. The First Amendment of the Constitution guarantees and protects these rights.

Question 7

How many amendments does the Constitution have?

Answer 7

- **27**

The first ten amendments to the Constitution are called the Bill of Rights. They were added in 1791. Since then, 17 more amendments have been added. The Constitution currently has 27 amendments. The 27th Amendment was added in 1992. It explains how senators and representatives are paid. Interestingly, Congress first discussed this amendment back in 1789 as one of the original amendments considered for the Bill of Rights.

Question 8

What did the Declaration of Independence do?

Answer 8

- **announced our independence
  (from Great Britain)**
- **declared our independence
  (from Great Britain)**
- **said that the United States is free
  (from Great Britain)**

The Declaration of Independence contains important
ideas about the American system of government. The
Declaration of Independence states that all people are
created equal and have "certain unalienable rights."
These are rights that no government can change or take
away. The author of the Declaration, Thomas Jefferson,
wrote that the American colonies should be independent
because Great Britain did not respect the basic rights
of people in the colonies. Jefferson believed that a
government exists only if the people think it should.
He believed in the idea that the people create their own
government and consent, or agree, to follow laws their
government makes. This idea is called "consent of the

(continued on p. 20)

The Declaration of Independence

(continued from p. 18)

governed." If the government creates laws that are fair and protect people, then people will agree to follow those laws. In the Declaration of Independence, Jefferson wrote a list of complaints the colonists had against the King of England. Jefferson ended the Declaration with the statement that the colonies are, and should be, free and independent states. The Second Continental Congress voted to accept the Declaration on July 4, 1776.

Question 9

What are two rights in the Declaration of Independence?

Answer 9

- **life**
- **liberty**
- **pursuit of happiness**

The Declaration of Independence lists three rights that the Founding Fathers considered to be natural and "unalienable." They are the right to life, liberty, and the pursuit of happiness. These ideas about freedom and individual rights were the basis for declaring America's independence. Thomas Jefferson and the other Founding Fathers believed that people are born with natural rights that no government can take away. Government exists to protect these rights. Because the people voluntarily give up power to a government, they can take that power back. The British government was not protecting the rights of the colonists, so the colonies took back their power and separated from Great Britain.

Question 10

What is freedom
of religion?

Answer 10

• You can practice any religion, or not practice a religion.

Colonists from Spain, France, Holland, England, and other countries came to America for many different reasons. One of the reasons was religious freedom. The rulers of many of these countries told their citizens that they must go to a certain church and worship in a certain way. Some people had different religious beliefs than their rulers and wanted to have their own churches. In 1620, the Pilgrims were the first group that came to America seeking religious freedom. Religious freedom was also important to the Framers. For this reason, freedom of religion was included in the Constitution as part of the Bill of Rights. The First Amendment to the Constitution guarantees freedom of religion. The First Amendment states, "Congress shall make no law respecting an establishment of religion, or prohibiting the free exercise thereof." The First Amendment also prohibits Congress from setting up an official U.S. religion, and protects citizens' rights to hold any religious belief, or none at all.

Question 11

What is the economic system in the United States?

Answer 11

- **capitalist economy**
- **market economy**

The economic system of the United States is capitalism. In the American economy, most businesses are privately owned. Competition and profit motivate businesses. Businesses and consumers interact in the marketplace, where prices can be negotiated. This is called a "market economy." In a market economy, businesses decide what to produce, how much to produce, and what to charge. Consumers decide what, when, and where they will buy goods or services. In a market economy, competition, supply, and demand influence the decisions of businesses and consumers.

Question 12

What is the "rule of law"?

Answer 12

- **Everyone must follow the law.**
- **Leaders must obey the law.**
- **Government must obey the law.**
- **No one is above the law.**

John Adams was one of the Founding Fathers and the second president of the United States. He wrote that our country is, "a government of laws, and not of men." No person or group is above the law. The rule of law means that everyone (citizens and leaders) must obey the laws. In the United States, the U.S. Constitution is the foundation for the rule of law. The United States is a "constitutional democracy" (a democracy with a constitution). In constitutional democracies, people are willing to obey the laws because the laws are made by the people through their elected representatives. If all people are governed by the same laws, the individual rights and liberties of each person are better protected. The rule of law helps to make sure that government protects all people equally and does not violate the rights of certain people.

PRINCIPLES OF AMERICAN DEMOCRACY

SYSTEM *of* GOVERNMENT

Question 13

Name one branch or part of the government.

Answer 13

- **executive**
- **judicial**
- **legislative**

The Constitution establishes three branches of government: legislative, executive, and judicial. Article I of the Constitution establishes the legislative branch. Article I explains that Congress makes laws. Congress (the Senate and the House of Representatives) is the legislative branch of the U.S. government. Article II of the Constitution establishes the executive branch. The executive branch enforces the laws that Congress passes. The executive branch makes sure all the people follow the laws of the United States. The president is the head of the executive branch. The vice president and members of the president's cabinet are also part of the executive branch. Article III of the Constitution establishes the judicial branch. The judicial branch places the highest judicial power in the Supreme Court. One responsibility of the judicial branch is to decide if government laws and actions follow the Constitution. This is a very important responsibility.

Question 14

What stops one branch of government from becoming too powerful?

Answer 14

- **checks and balances**
- **separation of powers**

The Constitution separates the government's power into three branches to prevent one person or group from having too much power. The separation of government into three branches creates a system of checks and balances. This means that each branch can block, or threaten to block, the actions of the other branches. Here are some examples: the Senate (part of the legislative branch) can block a treaty signed by the president (the executive branch). In this example, the legislative branch is "checking" the executive. The U.S. Supreme Court (the judicial branch) can reject a law passed by Congress (the legislative branch). In this example, the judicial branch is "checking" the legislative branch. This separation of powers limits the power of the government and prevents the government from violating the rights of the people.

Who is in charge of the executive branch?

Answer 15

• the president

The job of the executive branch is to carry out, or execute, federal laws and enforce laws passed by Congress. The head of the executive branch is the president. The president is both the head of state and the head of government. The president's powers include the ability to sign treaties with other countries and to select ambassadors to represent the United States around the world. The president also sets national policies and proposes laws to Congress. The president names the top leaders of the federal departments. When there is a vacancy on the Supreme Court, the president names a new member. However, the Senate has the power to reject the president's choices. This limit on the power of the president is an example of checks and balances.

Question 16

Who makes federal laws?

Answer 16

- **Congress**
- **Senate and House (of Representatives)**
- **(U.S. or national) legislature**

Congress makes federal laws. A federal law usually applies to all states and all people in the United States. Either side of Congress—the Senate or the House of Representatives—can propose a bill to address an issue. When the Senate proposes a bill, it sends the bill to a Senate committee. The Senate committee studies the issue and the bill. When the House of Representatives proposes a bill, it sends the bill to a House of Representatives committee. The committee studies the bill and sometimes makes changes to it. Then the bill goes to the full House or Senate for consideration. When each chamber passes its own version of the bill, it often goes to a "conference committee." The conference committee has members from both the House and the Senate. This committee discusses the bill, tries to resolve the differences, and writes a report with the final version

(continued on p. 40)

SYSTEM OF GOVERNMENT

(continued from p. 38)

of the bill. Then the committee sends the final version of the bill back to both houses for approval. If both houses approve the bill, it is considered "enrolled." An enrolled bill goes to the president to be signed into law. If the president signs the bill, it becomes a federal law.

Question 17

What are the two parts of the U.S. Congress?

Answer 17

- **the Senate and House (of Representatives)**

Congress is divided into two parts—the Senate and the House of Representatives. Because it has two "chambers," the U.S. Congress is known as a "bicameral" legislature. The system of checks and balances works in Congress. Specific powers are assigned to each of these chambers. For example, only the Senate has the power to reject a treaty signed by the president or a person the president chooses to serve on the Supreme Court. Only the House of Representatives has the power to introduce a bill that requires Americans to pay taxes.

Question 18

How many U.S. senators are there?

Answer 18

- **100**

There are 100 senators in Congress, two from each state. All states have equal power in the Senate because each state has the same number of senators. States with a very small population have the same number of senators as states with very large populations. The Framers of the Constitution made sure that the Senate would be small. This would keep it more orderly than the larger House of Representatives. As James Madison wrote in *Federalist Paper* #63, the Senate should be a "temperate and respectable body of citizens" that operates in a "cool and deliberate" way.

Question 19

We elect a U.S. senator for how many years?

Answer 19

- **6**

....

The Framers of the Constitution wanted senators to be independent from public opinion. They thought a fairly long, six-year term would give them this protection. They also wanted longer Senate terms to balance the shorter two-year terms of the members of the House, who would more closely follow public opinion. The Constitution puts no limit on the number of terms a senator may serve. Elections for U.S. senators take place on even-numbered years. Every two years, one-third of the senators are up for election.

Question 20

Who is one of your state's U.S. senators now?

Answer 20

- **Answers will vary. [The District of Columbia and U.S. territories have no U.S. Senators.]**

For a complete list of U.S. senators and the states they represent, go to www.senate.gov.

Chris van Hollen (D)
Ben Cardin (D)

Question 21

The House of Representatives has how many voting members?

Answer 21

- **435**

The House of Representatives is the larger chamber of Congress. Since 1912, the House of Representatives has had 435 voting members. However, the distribution of members among the states has changed over the years. Each state must have at least one representative in the House. Beyond that, the number of representatives from each state depends on the population of the state. The Constitution says that the government will conduct a census of the population every 10 years to count the number of people in each state. The results of the census are used to recalculate the number of representatives each state should have. For example, if one state gains many residents that state could get one or more new representatives. If another state loses residents, that state could lose one or more. But the total number of voting U.S. representatives does not change.

Question 22

We elect a U.S. representative for how many years?

Answer 22

- *2*

People who live in a representative's district are called "constituents." Representatives tend to reflect the views of their constituents. If representatives do not do this, they may be voted out of office. The Framers of the Constitution believed that short two-year terms and frequent elections would keep representatives close to their constituents, public opinion, and more aware of local and community concerns. The Constitution puts no limit on the number of terms a representative may serve. All representatives are up for election every two years.

Question 23

Name your U.S. representative.

Answer 23

- **Answers will vary. [The District of Columbia and U.S. territories have no (voting) Representatives in Congress.]**

For a complete list of U.S. representatives and the districts they represent, go to www.house.gov.

Question 24

Who does a U.S. senator represent?

Answer 24

- **all people of the state**

Senators are elected to serve the people of their state for six years. Each of the two senators represents the entire state. Before the 17th Amendment to the Constitution was ratified in 1913, the state legislatures elected the U.S. senators to represent their state. Now, all the voters in a state elect their two U.S. senators directly.

Question 25

Why do some states have more representatives than other states?

Answer 25

- **(because of) the state's population**
- **(because) they have more people**
- **(because) some states have more people**

....

The Founding Fathers wanted people in all states to be represented fairly. In the House of Representatives, a state's population determines the number of representatives it has. In this way, states with many people have a stronger voice in the House. In the Senate, every state has the same number of senators. This means that states with few people still have a strong voice in the national government.

Question 26

We elect a president for how many years?

Answer 26

- **4**

....

Early American leaders thought that the head of the
British government, the king, had too much power.
Because of this, they limited the powers of the head of
the new U.S. government. They decided that the people
would elect the president every four years. The president
is the only official elected by the entire country through
the Electoral College. The Electoral College is a process
that was designed by the writers of the Constitution to
select presidents. It came from a compromise between
the president being elected directly by the people and
the president being chosen by Congress. Citizens vote for
electors, who then choose the president. Before 1951, there
was no limit on the number of terms a president could
serve. With the 22nd Amendment to the Constitution,
the president can only be elected to two terms (four years
each) for a total of eight years.

Question 27

In what month do we vote for president?

Answer 27

- **November**

The Constitution did not set a national election day.
In the past, elections for federal office took place on
different days in different states. In 1845, Congress passed
legislation to designate a single day for all Americans
to vote. It made Election Day the Tuesday after the first
Monday in November. Congress chose November because
the United States was mostly rural. By November, farmers
had completed their harvests and were available to vote.
Another reason for this date was the weather. People
were able to travel because it was not yet winter. They
chose Tuesday for Election Day so that voters had a full
day after Sunday to travel to the polls.

Question 28

What is the name of the president of the United States now (in the year 2015)?

Answer 28

- **Barack Obama**
- **Obama**

....

Barack Obama is the 44th president of the United
States. After winning the presidential election of 2008,
he became the first African-American president of
the United States. He won a second term in 2012.
As president, he is the head of the executive branch.
As commander in chief, he is also in charge of the
military. Obama was born in Hawaii on August 4, 1961.
He graduated from Columbia University in New York.
Obama also studied law and graduated from Harvard
University in Massachusetts. He served as a U.S. senator
for the state of Illinois before being elected president.
President Obama's wife, called "the First Lady," is
Michelle Obama.

Question 29

What is the name of the vice president now (in the year 2015)?

Answer 29

- **Joseph R. Biden, Jr.**
- **Joe Biden**
- **Biden**

Joseph (Joe) R. Biden, Jr. is the 47th vice president of the United States. Biden was born November 20, 1942 in Pennsylvania. Later, his family moved to Delaware. He graduated from the University of Delaware in 1965. In 1968, he graduated from law school at Syracuse University in New York. From 1972–2009, Biden served as a U.S. senator for the state of Delaware. As vice president, Biden is president of the U.S. Senate and a top advisor to the president. Vice President Biden is married to Jill Biden.

Question 30

If the president can no longer serve, who becomes president?

Answer 30

- **the vice president**

If the president dies, resigns, or cannot work while still in office, the vice president becomes president. For this reason, the qualifications for vice president and president are the same. A vice president became president nine times in U.S. history when the president died or left office. William Henry Harrison died in office in 1841. Zachary Taylor died in office in 1850. Abraham Lincoln was killed in office in 1865. James Garfield was killed in office in 1881. William McKinley was killed in office in 1901. Warren Harding died in office in 1923. Franklin Roosevelt died in office in 1945. John F. Kennedy was killed in office in 1963. Richard Nixon resigned from office in 1974. No one other than the vice president has ever succeeded to the presidency.

Question 31

If both the president and the vice president can no longer serve, who becomes president?

Answer 31

• the Speaker of the House

If both the president and vice president cannot serve, the next person in line is the speaker of the House of Representatives. This has not always been the procedure. Soon after the country was founded, a law was passed that made the Senate president pro tempore the next in line after the president and vice president. The president pro tempore presides over the Senate when the vice president is not there. Later in U.S. history, the secretary of state was third in line. With the Presidential Succession Act of 1947, Congress returned to the original idea of having a congressional leader next in line. In 1967, the 25th Amendment was ratified. It established procedures for presidential and vice presidential succession.

Question 32

Who is the commander in chief of the military?

Answer 32

- **the president**

The Founding Fathers strongly believed in republican ideals.
A republic is a government where a country's political power
comes from the citizens, not the rulers, and is put into use
by representatives elected by the citizens. That is why they
made the president the commander in chief. They wanted
a civilian selected by the people. They did not want a
professional military leader. The president commands the
armed forces, but Congress has the power to pay for the
armed forces and declare war. In 1973, many members of
Congress believed that the president was misusing or
abusing his powers as commander in chief. They thought
that the president was ignoring the legislative branch and
not allowing the system of checks and balances to work.
In response, Congress passed the War Powers Act. The
War Powers Act gave Congress a stronger voice in decisions
about the use of U.S. troops. President Richard Nixon
vetoed this bill, but Congress overrode his veto. Because
we have a system of checks and balances, one branch of
government is able to check the other branches.

Question 33

Who signs bills to become laws?

Answer 33

- **the president**

Every law begins as a proposal made by a member of Congress, either a senator (member of the Senate) or representative (member of the House of Representatives). When the Senate or House begins to debate the proposal, it is called a "bill." After debate in both houses of Congress, if a majority of both the Senate and House vote to pass the bill, it goes to the president. If the president wants the bill to become law, he signs it. If the president does not want the bill to become law, he vetoes it. The president cannot introduce a bill. If he has an idea for a bill, he must ask a member of Congress to introduce it.

Question 34

Who vetoes bills?

Answer 34

- **the president**

The president has veto power. This means that the president can reject a bill passed by Congress. If the president vetoes a bill, he prevents it from becoming a law. The president can send the bill back to Congress unsigned. Often he will list reasons why he rejects it. The president has ten days to evaluate the bill. If the president does not sign the bill after ten days and Congress is in session, the bill automatically becomes a law. If the president does nothing with the bill and Congress adjourns within the ten-day period, the bill does not become law—this is called a "pocket veto." If two-thirds of the House and two-thirds of the Senate vote to pass the bill again, the bill becomes a law, even though the president did not sign it. This process is called "overriding the president's veto." It is not easy to do.

Question 35

What does the president's cabinet do?

Answer 35

- **advises the president**

The Constitution says that the leaders of the executive departments should advise the president. These department leaders, most of them called "secretaries," make up the cabinet. The president nominates the cabinet members to be his advisors. For a nominee to be confirmed, a majority of the Senate must approve the nominee. Throughout history, presidents have been able to change who makes up the cabinet or add departments to the cabinet. For example, when the Department of Homeland Security was created, President George W. Bush added the leader of this department to his cabinet.

Question 36

What are two cabinet-level positions?

Answer 36

- Secretary of Agriculture
- Secretary of Commerce
- Secretary of Defense
- Secretary of Education
- Secretary of Energy
- Secretary of Health and Human Services
- Secretary of Homeland Security

- **Secretary of Housing and Urban Development**
- **Secretary of the Interior**
- **Secretary of Labor**
- **Secretary of State**
- **Secretary of Transportation**
- **Secretary of the Treasury**
- **Secretary of Veterans Affairs**
- **Attorney General**
- **vice president**

(continued from p. 80)

The people on the president's cabinet are the vice president and the heads of the 15 executive departments. The president may appoint other government officials to the cabinet. When George Washington was president, there were only four cabinet members: the secretary of state, secretary of the treasury, secretary of war, and attorney general. The government established the other executive departments later.

Question 37

What does the judicial branch do?

Answer 37

- reviews laws
- explains laws
- resolves disputes (disagreements)
- decides if a law goes against the
  Constitution

....

The judicial branch is one of the three branches of
government. The Constitution established the judicial
branch of government with the creation of the Supreme
Court. Congress created the other federal courts. All
these courts together make up the judicial branch. The
courts review and explain the laws, and they resolve
disagreements about the meaning of the law. The U.S.
Supreme Court makes sure that laws are consistent with
the Constitution. If a law is not consistent with the
Constitution, the Court can declare it unconstitutional.
In this case, the Court rejects the law. The Supreme
Court makes the final decision about all cases that have
to do with federal laws and treaties. It also rules on other
cases, such as disagreements between states.

Question 38

What is the highest court in the United States?

Answer 38

- **the Supreme Court**

The U.S. Supreme Court has complete authority over all federal courts. Its rulings have a significant effect. A Supreme Court ruling can affect the outcome of many cases in the lower courts. The Supreme Court's interpretations of federal laws and of the Constitution are final. The Supreme Court is limited in its power over the states. It cannot make decisions about state law or state constitutions. The Court can decide that a state law or action conflicts with federal law or with the U.S. Constitution. If this happens, the state law becomes invalid. The Supreme Court case ruling *Marbury v. Madison* established this power, known as "judicial review." The Supreme Court also rules on cases about significant social and public policy issues that affect all Americans. The Supreme Court ruled on the court case *Brown v. the Board of Education of Topeka*, which ended racial segregation in schools.

Question 39

How many justices are on the Supreme Court?

Answer 39

- **9**

The Constitution does not establish the number of justices on the Supreme Court. In the past, there have been as many as ten and as few as six justices. Now, there are nine justices on the Supreme Court: eight associate justices and one chief justice. The Constitution gives the president the power to nominate justices to the Supreme Court. The nominee must then be confirmed by the Senate. Justices serve on the court for life or until they retire. For more information on the Supreme Court, go to www.supremecourt.gov.

Question 40

Who is the chief justice of the United States now (in the year 2015)?

Answer 40

- ### John Roberts (John G. Roberts, Jr.)

John G. Roberts, Jr. is the 17th chief justice of the United States. After the death of former chief justice William Rehnquist in September 2005, President George W. Bush nominated Roberts for this position. Judge Roberts became chief justice when he was 50. He is the youngest chief justice since 1801, when John Marshall became chief justice at the age of 45. Before he became chief justice, Judge Roberts served on the U.S. Court of Appeals for the District of Columbia Circuit. Although the chief justice of the United States is the highest official in the judicial branch, his vote on the Supreme Court carries the same weight as the other justices.

Under our
Constitution, some
powers belong
to the federal
government.
What is one power
of the federal
government?

Answer 41

- **to print money**
- **to declare war**
- **to create an army**
- **to make treaties**

The powers of government are divided between the federal government and the state governments. The federal government is known as a limited government. Its powers are restricted to those described in the U.S. Constitution. The Constitution gives the federal government the power to print money, declare war, create an army, and make treaties with other nations. Most other powers that are not given to the federal government in the Constitution belong to the states.

Question 42

Under our Constitution, some powers belong to the states. What is one power of the states?

Answer 42

- **provide schooling and education**
- **provide protection (police)**
- **provide safety (fire departments)**
- **give a driver's license**
- **approve zoning and land use**

In the United States, the federal and state governments both hold power. Before the Constitution, the 13 colonies governed themselves individually much like state governments. It was not until the Articles of Confederation and then the Constitution that a national or federal government was established. Today, although each state has its own constitution, these state constitutions cannot conflict with the U.S. Constitution. The U.S. Constitution is the supreme law of the land. The state governments hold powers not given to the federal government in the U.S. Constitution. Some powers of the state government are the power to create traffic regulations and marriage requirements, and to issue driver's licenses. The Constitution also provides a list of powers that the states do not have. For example, states cannot coin (create) money. The state and federal governments also share some powers, such as the ability to tax people.

Question 43

Who is the governor of your state now?

Answer 43

- **Answers will vary. [District of Columbia residents should answer that D.C. does not have a governor.]**

To learn the name of the governor of your state or territory, go to www.nga.org/governors. Similar to the federal government, most states have three branches of government. The branches are executive, legislative, and judicial. The governor is the chief executive of the state. The governor's job in a state government is similar to the president's job in the federal government. However, the state laws that a governor carries out are different from the federal laws that the president carries out. The Constitution says that certain issues are covered by federal, not state, laws. All other issues are covered by state laws. The governor's duties and powers vary from state to state. The number of years that a governor is elected to serve—called a "term"—is four years. The exceptions are New Hampshire and Vermont, where governors serve for two years.

Question 44

What is the capital of your state?

Answer 44

- **Answers will vary. [District of Columbia residents should answer that D.C. is not a state and does not have a capital. Residents of U.S. territories should name the capital of the territory.]**

To learn the capital of your state or territory, go to http://bensguide.gpo.gov/3-5/state/index.html. Each state or territory has its own capital. The state capital is where the state government conducts its business. It is similar to the nation's capital, Washington, D.C., where the federal government conducts its business. Some state capitals have moved from one city to another over the years, but the state capitals have not changed since 1910. Usually, the governor lives in the state's capital city.

Question 45

What are the two major political parties in the United States?

Answer 45

- **Democratic and Republican**

The Constitution did not establish political parties. President George Washington specifically warned against them. But early in U.S. history, two political groups developed. They were the Democratic-Republicans and the Federalists. Today, the two major political parties are the Democratic Party and the Republican Party. President Andrew Jackson created the Democratic Party from the Democratic-Republicans. The Republican Party took over from the Whigs as a major party in the 1860s. The first Republican president was Abraham Lincoln. Throughout U.S. history, there have been other parties. These parties have included the Know-Nothing (also called American Party), Bull-Moose (also called Progressive), Reform, and Green parties. They have played various roles in American politics. Political party membership in the United States is voluntary. Parties are made up of people who organize to promote their candidates for election and to promote their views about public policies.

Question 46

What is the political party of the president now (in the year 2015)?

Answer 46

• Democratic (Party)

The two major political parties in the United States today are the Democratic and Republican parties. The current president, Barack Obama, is a member of the Democratic Party. Other notable Democratic presidents include Woodrow Wilson, Franklin D. Roosevelt, Harry Truman, John F. Kennedy, Lyndon B. Johnson, Jimmy Carter, and William "Bill" Clinton. Notable Republican presidents include Abraham Lincoln, Theodore Roosevelt, Warren Harding, Herbert Hoover, Dwight Eisenhower, Ronald Reagan, and George H. W. Bush. Since the middle of the 19th century, the symbol of the Republican Party has been the elephant. The Republican Party is also known as the "Grand Old Party" or the "GOP." The symbol of the Democratic Party is the donkey.

Question 47

What is the name of the speaker of the House of Representatives now (in the year 2015)?

Answer 47

• (John) Boehner

The current speaker of the House of Representatives is John Boehner. He has represented Ohio's Eighth District in the House of Representatives since 1991. As speaker, he presides over the House of Representatives and leads the majority political party in the House, the Republican Party. The speaker is second in line to the succession of the presidency after the vice president. Frederick Muhlenberg, of Pennsylvania (pictured at right), was elected the first speaker in 1789.

SYSTEM OF GOVERNMENT

105

RIGHTS *and* RESPONSIBILITIES

Question 48

There are four amendments to the Constitution about who can vote. Describe one of them.

Answer 48

- **Citizens 18 and older (can vote).**
- **You don't have to pay (a poll tax) to vote.**
- **Any citizen can vote. (Women and men can vote.)**
- **A male citizen of any race (can vote).**

Voting is one of the most important civic responsibilities of citizens in the United States. In a democratic society, the people choose the leaders who will represent them. There are four amendments to the Constitution about voting. The 15th Amendment permits American men of all races to vote. It was written after the Civil War and the end of slavery. The 19th Amendment gave women the right to vote. It resulted from the women's suffrage movement (the women's rights movement). After the 15th Amendment was passed, some leaders of the southern states were upset that African Americans could vote. These leaders designed fees called poll taxes to stop them from voting. The 24th Amendment made these poll taxes illegal. The 26th Amendment lowered the voting age from 21 to 18.

Question 49

What is one responsibility that is only for United States citizens?

Answer 49

- **serve on a jury**
- **vote in a federal election**

Two responsibilities of U.S. citizens are to serve on a jury and vote in federal elections. The Constitution gives citizens the right to a trial by a jury. The jury is made up of U.S. citizens. Participation of citizens on a jury helps ensure a fair trial. Another important responsibility of citizens is voting. The law does not require citizens to vote, but voting is a very important part of any democracy. By voting, citizens are participating in the democratic process. Citizens vote for leaders to represent them and their ideas, and the leaders support the citizens' interests.

Question 50

Name one right only for United States citizens.

Answer 50

- **vote in a federal election**
- **run for federal office**

U.S. citizens have the right to vote in federal elections. Permanent residents can vote in local or state elections that do not require voters to be U.S. citizens. Only U.S. citizens can vote in federal elections. U.S. citizens can also run for federal office. Qualifications to run for the Senate or House of Representatives include being a U.S. citizen for a certain number of years. A candidate for Senate must have been a U.S. citizen for at least nine years. A candidate for the House must have been a U.S. citizen for at least seven years. To run for president of the United States, a candidate must be a native-born (not naturalized) citizen. In addition to the benefits of citizenship, U.S. citizens have certain responsibilities—to respect the law, stay informed on issues, participate in the democratic process, and pay their taxes.

Question 51

What are two rights of everyone living in the United States?

Answer 51

- **freedom of expression**
- **freedom of speech**
- **freedom of assembly**
- **freedom to petition the government**
- **freedom of worship**
- **the right to bear arms**

Thomas Jefferson said, "[The] best principles [of our republic] secure to all its citizens a perfect equality of rights." Millions of immigrants have come to America to have these rights. The Constitution and the Bill of Rights give many of these rights to all people living in the United States. These rights include the freedom of expression, of religion, of speech, and the right to bear arms. All people living in the United States also have many of the same duties as citizens, such as paying taxes and obeying the laws.

Question 52

What do we show loyalty to when we say the Pledge of Allegiance?

Answer 52

- **the United States**
- **the flag**

The flag is an important symbol of the United States. The Pledge of Allegiance to the flag states, "I pledge allegiance to the Flag of the United States of America and to the Republic for which it stands, one Nation, under God, indivisible, with liberty and justice for all." When we say the Pledge of Allegiance, we usually stand facing the flag with the right hand over the heart. Francis Bellamy wrote the pledge. It was first published in *The Youth's Companion* magazine in 1892 for children to say on the anniversary of Columbus's discovery of America. Congress officially recognized the pledge on June 22, 1942. Two changes have been made since it was written in 1892. "I pledge allegiance to my flag" was changed to "I pledge allegiance to the Flag of the United States of America." Congress added the phrase "under God" on June 14, 1954.

Question 53

What is one promise you make when you become a United States citizen?

Answer 53

- **give up loyalty to other countries**
- **defend the Constitution and laws of the United States**
- **obey the laws of the United States**
- **serve in the U.S. military (if needed)**
- **serve (do important work for) the nation (if needed)**
- **be loyal to the United States**

When the United States became an independent country, the Constitution gave Congress the power to establish a uniform rule of naturalization. Congress made rules about how immigrants could become citizens. Many of these requirements are still valid today, such as the requirements to live in the United States for a specific period of time, to be of good moral character, and to understand and support the principles of the Constitution. After an immigrant fulfills all of the requirements to become a U.S. citizen, the final step is to take an Oath of Allegiance at a naturalization ceremony. The Oath of Allegiance states:

(continued on p. 120)

RIGHTS AND RESPONSIBILITIES

119

(continued from p. 118)

I hereby declare, on oath, that I absolutely and entirely renounce and abjure all allegiance and fidelity to any foreign prince, potentate, state, or sovereignty of whom or which I have heretofore been a subject or citizen; that I will support and defend the Constitution and laws of the United States of America against all enemies, foreign and domestic; that I will bear true faith and allegiance to the same; that I will bear arms on behalf of the United States when required by the law; that I will perform noncombatant service in the Armed Forces of the United States when required by the law; that I will perform work of national importance under civilian direction when required by the law; and that I take this obligation freely without any mental reservation or purpose of evasion; so help me God.

Question 54

How old do citizens have to be to vote for president?

Answer 54

- **18 or older**

For most of U.S. history, Americans had to be at least 21 years old to vote. At the time of the Vietnam War, during the 1960s and 1970s, many people thought that people who were old enough to fight in a war should also be old enough to vote. In 1971, the 26th Amendment changed the minimum voting age from 21 to 18 for all federal, state, and local elections. The National Voter Registration Act of 1993 made it easier for people to register to vote. Now they can register to vote by mail, at public assistance offices, or when they apply for or renew their driver's license.

Question 55

What are two ways that Americans can participate in their democracy?

Answer 55

- vote
- join a political party
- help with a campaign
- join a civic group
- join a community group
- give an elected official your opinion
  on an issue
- call Senators and Representatives
- publicly support or oppose an issue
- run for office
- write to a newspaper

Citizens play an active part in their communities. When Americans engage in the political process, democracy stays alive and strong. There are many ways for people to be involved. They can volunteer to help new immigrants learn English and civics, join the Parent Teacher Association (PTA) of their child's school, run for a position on the local school board, or volunteer to help at a polling station. People can also vote, help with a political campaign, join a civic or community organization, or call their senator or representative about an issue that is important to them.

When is the last day you can send in federal income tax forms?

Answer 56

- **April 15**

The last day to send in your federal income tax to the Internal Revenue Service is April 15 of each year. The Constitution gave the federal government the power to collect taxes. The federal government needs money to pay the nation's debts and to defend and provide for the needs of the country. When the country was young, it was difficult to raise money from the 13 original states. The government began collecting income tax for the first time through the Revenue Act of 1861. This was only temporary. In 1894, a flat-rate federal income tax was enacted, but the Supreme Court said this was unconstitutional. Finally, in 1913, the 16th Amendment was ratified. It gave Congress the power to collect income taxes. Today, "taxable income" is money that is earned from wages, self-employment, tips, and the sale of property. The government uses these taxes to keep our country safe and secure. It also tries to cure and prevent diseases through research. In addition, the government uses these taxes to educate children and adults, and build and repair our roads and highways. Taxes are used to do these things and many more.

Question 57

When must all men register for the Selective Service?

Answer 57

- **at age 18**
- **between 18 and 26**

....

President Lincoln tried to draft men to fight during the Civil War, but many people became angry and rioted. In 1917, Congress passed the Selective Service Act. This act gave President Woodrow Wilson the power to temporarily increase the U.S. military during World War I. In 1940, President Franklin Roosevelt signed the Selective Training and Service Act, which created the first draft during peacetime. This was the beginning of the Selective Service System in the United States today. The draft was needed again for the Korean and Vietnam Wars. Today, there is no draft, but all men between 18 and 26 years old must register with the Selective Service System. When a man registers, he tells the government that he is available to serve in the U.S. Armed Forces. He can register at a United States post office or on the Internet. To register for Selective Service on the Internet, visit the Selective Service website at www.sss.gov.

American History

For more than 200 years, the United States has strived to become a "more perfect union." Its history has been one of expansive citizenship for all Americans. By learning about our shared history, you will be able to understand our nation's traditions, milestones, and common civic values. Our country is independent because of the strength, unity, and determination of our forefathers. It is important for future Americans to know this story. We are people working toward great ideals and principles guided by equality and fairness. This is important to keep our country free. As Americans, we have been committed to each other and our country throughout our history. The following section will help you understand American history from the colonial period and independence to the Civil War and other important events during the 1800s, 1900s, and today.

COLONIAL PERIOD *and* INDEPENDENCE

Question 58

What is one reason colonists came to America?

Answer 58

- **freedom**
- **political liberty**
- **religious freedom**
- **economic opportunity**
- **practice their religion**
- **escape persecution**

In the 1600s and 1700s, colonists from England and other European countries sailed across the Atlantic Ocean to the American colonies. Some left Europe to escape religious restrictions or persecution, to practice their religion freely. Many came for political freedom, and some came for economic opportunity. These freedoms and opportunities often did not exist in the colonists' home countries. For these settlers, the American colonies were a chance for freedom and a new life. Today, many people come to the United States for these same reasons.

Question 59

Who lived in America before the Europeans arrived?

Answer 59

- **American Indians**
- **Native Americans**

Great American Indian tribes such as the Navajo, Sioux, Cherokee, and Iroquois lived in America at the time the Pilgrims arrived. The Pilgrims settled in an area where a tribe called the Wampanoag lived. The Wampanoag taught the Pilgrims important skills, such as how to farm with different methods and how to grow crops such as corn, beans, and squash. Relations with some American Indian tribes became tense and confrontational as more Europeans moved to America and migrated west. Eventually, after much violence, the settlers defeated those American Indian tribes and took much of their land.

Question 60

What group of people was taken to America and sold as slaves?

Answer 60

- **Africans**
- **people from Africa**

Slavery existed in many countries long before America was founded. By 1700, many Africans were being brought to the American colonies as slaves. Men, women, and children were brought against their will. They were often separated from their families when they were sold as slaves. Slaves worked without payment and without basic rights. Most worked in agriculture, but slaves did many other kinds of work in the colonies, too. Slavery created a challenge for a nation founded on individual freedoms and democratic beliefs. It was one of the major causes of the American Civil War.

Question 61

Why did the colonists fight the British?

Answer 61

- **because of high taxes (taxation without representation)**
- **because the British army stayed in their houses (boarding, quartering)**
- **because they didn't have self-government**

....

The American colonists' anger had been growing for years before the Revolutionary War began in 1775. The decision to separate from the British was not an easy choice for many colonists. However, Great Britain's "repeated injuries" against the Americans, as noted in the Declaration of Independence, convinced many to join the rebellion. The British taxed the colonists without their consent, and the colonists had nobody to represent their needs and ideas to the British government. They were also angry because ordinary colonists were forced to let British soldiers sleep and eat in their homes. The colonists believed the British did not respect their basic rights. The British governed the colonists without their consent, denying them self-government.

Question 62

Who wrote the Declaration of Independence?

Answer 62

- **(Thomas) Jefferson**

Thomas Jefferson wrote the Declaration of Independence in 1776. He was a very important political leader and thinker. Some of the most important ideas about the American government are found in the Declaration of Independence, such as the idea that all people are created equal. Another important idea is that people are born with certain rights including life, liberty, and the pursuit of happiness. Jefferson was the third president of the United States, serving from 1801 to 1809. Before becoming president, Jefferson was governor of Virginia and the first U.S. secretary of state. He strongly supported individual rights, especially freedom of religion. Jefferson wanted to protect these rights. For this reason, he did not want a strong national government.

Question 63

When was the Declaration of Independence adopted?

Answer 63

- **July 4, 1776**

In 1774, representatives from 12 of the 13 colonies met in Philadelphia, Pennsylvania, for the First Continental Congress. Of the 13 colonies, only Georgia was absent. These representatives were angry about British laws that treated them unfairly. They began to organize an army. The Second Continental Congress met in 1775 after fighting began between the colonists and the British Army. This Congress asked Thomas Jefferson and others to write the Declaration of Independence. When Thomas Jefferson finished his draft of the Declaration of Independence, he took it to John Adams, Benjamin Franklin, and the others on the committee to review it. After changes were made by the committee, the Declaration was read to the members of the entire Congress. The purpose of the Declaration was to announce the separation of the colonies from England. The Declaration of Independence stated that if a government does not protect the rights of the people, the people can create a new government. For this reason, the colonists separated from their British rulers. On July 4, 1776, the Second Continental Congress adopted the Declaration of Independence.

Question 64

There were 13 original states. Name three.

Answer 64

- **New Hampshire**
- **Massachusetts**
- **Rhode Island**
- **Connecticut**
- **New York**
- **New Jersey**
- **Pennsylvania**
- **Delaware**
- **Maryland**
- **Virginia**
- **North Carolina**
- **South Carolina**
- **Georgia**

The 13 original states were all former British colonies. Representatives from these colonies came together and declared independence from Great Britain in 1776. After the Revolutionary War, the colonies became free and independent states. When the 13 colonies became

(continued on p. 146)

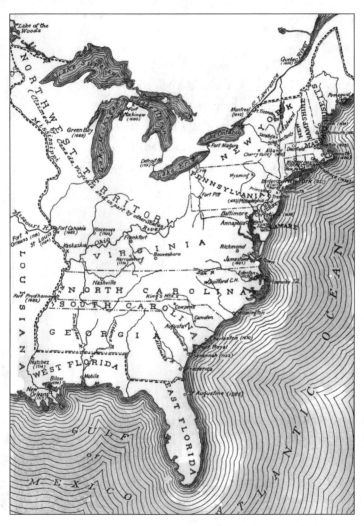

COLONIAL PERIOD AND INDEPENDENCE

(continued from p. 144)

states, each state set up its own government. They wrote state constitutions. Eventually, the people in these states created a new form of national government that would unite all the states into a single nation under the U.S. Constitution. The first three colonies to become states were Delaware, Pennsylvania, and New Jersey. This happened in 1787. Eight colonies became states in 1788. These were Georgia, Connecticut, Massachusetts, Maryland, South Carolina, New Hampshire, Virginia, and New York. North Carolina became a state in 1789. Rhode Island became a state in 1790. Although the colonies were recognized as states after the Declaration of Independence, the date of statehood is based on when they ratified (accepted) the U.S. Constitution. Today, the United States has 50 states.

Question 65

What happened at the Constitutional Convention?

Answer 65

1787

- **The Constitution was written.**
- **The Founding Fathers wrote the Constitution.**

....

The Constitutional Convention was held in Philadelphia, Pennsylvania, from May to September 1787. Fifty-five delegates from 12 of the original 13 states (except for Rhode Island) met to write amendments to the Articles of Confederation. The delegates met because many American leaders did not like the Articles. The national government under the Articles of Confederation was not strong enough. Instead of changing the Articles of Confederation, the delegates decided to create a new governing document with a stronger national government—the Constitution. Each state sent delegates, who worked for four months in secret to allow for free and open discussion as they wrote the new document. The delegates who attended the Constitutional Convention are called "the Framers." On September 17, 1787, 39 of the delegates signed the new Constitution.

Question 66

When was the Constitution written?

Answer 66

- **1787**

....

The Constitution, written in 1787, created a new system
of U.S. government—the same system we have today.
James Madison was the main writer of the Constitution.
He became the fourth president of the United States.
The U.S. Constitution is short, but it defines the
principles of government and the rights of citizens in
the United States. The document has a preamble and
seven articles. Since its adoption, the Constitution
has been amended (changed) 27 times. Three-fourths
of the states (nine of the original 13) were required to
ratify (approve) the Constitution. Delaware was the first
state to ratify the Constitution on December 7, 1787.
In 1788, New Hampshire was the ninth state to ratify
the Constitution. On March 4, 1789, the Constitution
took effect and Congress met for the first time. George
Washington was inaugurated as president the same year.
By 1790, all 13 states had ratified the Constitution.

Question 67

The Federalist Papers supported the passage of the U.S. Constitution. Name one of the writers.

Answer 67

- **(James) Madison**
- **(Alexander) Hamilton**
- **(John) Jay**
- **Publius**

The Federalist Papers were 85 essays that were printed in New York newspapers while New York State was deciding whether or not to support the U.S. Constitution. The essays were written in 1787 and 1788 by Alexander Hamilton, John Jay, and James Madison under the pen name "Publius." The essays explained why the state should ratify the Constitution. Other newspapers outside New York also published the essays as other states were deciding to ratify the Constitution. In 1788, the papers were published together in a book called *The Federalist*. Today, people still read the Federalist Papers to help them understand the Constitution.

Question 68

What is one thing Benjamin Franklin is famous for?

Answer 68

- **U.S. diplomat**
- **oldest member of the Constitutional Convention**
- **first postmaster general of the United States**
- **writer of *Poor Richard's Almanac***
- **started the first free libraries**

Benjamin Franklin was one of the most influential Founding Fathers of the United States. He was the oldest delegate to the Constitutional Convention and one of the signers of the U.S. Constitution. He was a printer, author, politician, diplomat, and inventor. By his mid–20s, he was an accomplished printer, and he began writing books and papers. Franklin's most famous publication was *Poor Richard's Almanac*. He also organized America's first library. Its members loaned books to one another. He was very active in colonial politics. He also visited England and France many times as a U.S. diplomat. In 1775, the Second Continental Congress appointed Franklin the first postmaster general.

Question 69

Who is the "Father of Our Country"?

Answer 69

• (George) Washington

George Washington is called the Father of Our Country. He was the first American president. Before that, he was a brave general who led the Continental Army to victory over Great Britain during the American Revolutionary War. After his victory over the British Army, Washington retired to his farm in Virginia named Mount Vernon. He left retirement to help create the new country's system of government. He presided over the Constitutional Convention in Philadelphia in 1787.

Question 70

Who was the first President?

Answer 70

- **(George) Washington**

George Washington was the first president of the United States. He began his first term in 1789. He served for a second term beginning in 1793. Washington played an important role in forming the new nation and encouraged Americans to unite. He also helped define the American presidency. He voluntarily resigned from the presidency after two terms. He set an example for future leaders in his own country and the world by voluntarily giving up power. The tradition of a president serving no more than two terms continued in the United States until Franklin D. Roosevelt, who was elected to office four times (1933–1945). The 22nd Amendment to the Constitution, passed in 1947, now limits presidents to two terms.

COLONIAL PERIOD AND INDEPENDENCE

159

1800s

Question 71

What territory did the United States buy from France in 1803?

Answer 71

- **the Louisiana Territory**
- **Louisiana**

The Louisiana Territory was a large area west of the Mississippi River. It was 828,000 square miles. In 1803, the United States bought the Louisiana Territory from France for $15 million. The Louisiana Purchase Treaty was signed in Paris on April 30, 1803. It was the largest acquisition of land in American history. Farmers could now ship their farm products down the Mississippi River without permission from other countries. This was important because the city of New Orleans was a major shipping port. The Louisiana Purchase doubled the size of the United States and expanded it westward. Meriwether Lewis and William Clark led an 1804 expedition to map the Louisiana Territory.

Question 72

Name one war fought by the United States in the 1800s.

Answer 72

- **War of 1812**
- **Mexican-American War**
- **Civil War**
- **Spanish-American War**

The United States fought four major wars in the 1800s—the War of 1812, the Mexican-American War, the Civil War, and the Spanish-American War.

The War of 1812 lasted from 1812 through 1815. President James Madison asked Congress to declare war on Great Britain. The British were stopping and seizing American ships. They were also arming American Indians to fight against the Americans. As a result of this war, the nation's trade was disrupted and the U.S. Capitol was burned. The Americans won the war. This was the first time after the Revolutionary War that America had to fight a foreign country to protect its independence.

The Mexican-American War was a conflict between Mexico and America. The war began in Texas in 1846. President James Polk ordered General Zachary Taylor and his forces to occupy land claimed by both the United States and Mexico. President Polk believed westward expansion was important for the United States to grow. When Mexico attacked, the United States went to war with Mexico. When the war ended in February 1848, the United States and Mexico signed the Treaty of Guadalupe Hidalgo. This treaty gave Texas to the United States and extended the boundaries of the United States west to the Pacific Ocean.

In the Civil War, the people of the United States fought against each other. Americans in the northern states fought to support the federal government ("the Union") against Americans from the southern states. The southern states were trying to separate themselves to form a new nation, the Confederate States of America ("the Confederacy"). The war lasted from 1861 to 1865, when the Confederate army surrendered to the Union army. Many lives were lost in the American Civil War.

In 1898, the United States fought Spain in the Spanish-American War. The United States wanted to help Cuba become independent from Spain because the United States had economic interests in Cuba. The war began when a U.S. battleship was sunk near Cuba. Many Americans believed it was the Spanish who attacked the ship. For this reason, America went to war with Spain. By the end of 1898, the war was over with a victory for the United States. Cuba had its independence, and Guam, Puerto Rico, and the Philippines became territories of the United States.

Question 73

What was the name of the U.S. war between the North and the South?

Answer 73

- **the Civil War**
- **the War between the States**

The American Civil War is also known as the War between the States. It was a war between the people in the northern states and those in the southern states. The Civil War was fought in many places across the United States, but most battles were fought in the southern states. The first battle was at Fort Sumter, South Carolina. The first major battle between the northern (Union) army and the southern (Confederate) army took place at Bull Run, in Manassas, Virginia, in July 1861. The Union expected the war to end quickly. After its defeat at the Battle of Bull Run, the Union realized that the war would be long and difficult. In 1865, the Civil War ended with the capture of the Confederate capital in Richmond, Virginia. Confederate General Robert E. Lee surrendered to Lt. General Ulysses S. Grant of the Union army at Appomattox Courthouse in central Virginia. Over the four-year period, more than 3 million Americans fought in the Civil War and more than 600,000 people died.

Question 74

What was one problem that led to the Civil War?

Answer 74

- **slavery**
- **economic reasons**
- **states' rights**

The Civil War began when 11 southern states voted to secede (separate) from the United States to form their own country, the Confederate States of America. These southern states believed that the federal government of the United States threatened their right to make their own decisions. They wanted states' rights with each state making its own decisions about its government. If the national government contradicted the state, they did not want to follow the national government. The North and South had very different economic systems. The South's agriculture-based economy depended heavily on slave labor. The southern states feared that the United States government would end slavery. The southern states believed that this would hurt their economic and political independence. The economy of the northern states was more industrial and did not depend on slavery.

(continued on p. 172)

1800s

171

(continued from p. 170)

The northern states fought to keep all the United States together in "the Union." They tried to stop the southern states from separating into a new Confederate nation. There were also many people in the North who wanted to end slavery. These differences led to the American Civil War, which lasted from 1861 until 1865.

Question 75

What was one important thing that Abraham Lincoln did?

Answer 75

- **freed the slaves (Emancipation Proclamation)**
- **saved (or preserved) the Union**
- **led the United States during the Civil War**

Abraham Lincoln was president of the United States from 1861 to 1865, and led the nation during the Civil War. Lincoln thought the separation of the southern (Confederate) states was unconstitutional, and he wanted to preserve the Union. In 1863, during the Civil War, he issued the Emancipation Proclamation. It declared that the slaves who lived in the rebelling Confederate states were forever free. Lincoln is also famous for his "Gettysburg Address." He gave that speech at Gettysburg, Pennsylvania, in November 1863. Earlier that year, at the Battle of Gettysburg, the northern (Union) army had won a major battle to stop the Confederate army from invading the North. To honor the many who died in this battle, the governor of Pennsylvania established the

(continued on p. 176)

Question 75

What was one important thing that Abraham Lincoln did?

Answer 75

- **freed the slaves (Emancipation Proclamation)**
- **saved (or preserved) the Union**
- **led the United States during the Civil War**

Abraham Lincoln was president of the United States from 1861 to 1865, and led the nation during the Civil War. Lincoln thought the separation of the southern (Confederate) states was unconstitutional, and he wanted to preserve the Union. In 1863, during the Civil War, he issued the Emancipation Proclamation. It declared that the slaves who lived in the rebelling Confederate states were forever free. Lincoln is also famous for his "Gettysburg Address." He gave that speech at Gettysburg, Pennsylvania, in November 1863. Earlier that year, at the Battle of Gettysburg, the northern (Union) army had won a major battle to stop the Confederate army from invading the North. To honor the many who died in this battle, the governor of Pennsylvania established the

(continued on p. 176)

1800s

175

(continued from p. 174)

Soldiers' National Cemetery at Gettysburg. Lincoln spoke at the dedication ceremony and praised those who fought and died in battle. He asked those still living to rededicate themselves to saving the Union so that "government of the people, by the people, for the people shall not perish from the earth." On April 14, 1865, soon after taking office for his second term, Abraham Lincoln was killed by a southern supporter, John Wilkes Booth, at Ford's Theatre in Washington, D.C.

Question 76

What did the Emancipation Proclamation do?

Answer 76

- **freed the slaves**
- **freed slaves in the Confederacy**
- **freed slaves in the Confederate states**
- **freed slaves in most Southern states**

In 1863, in the middle of the Civil War, President Abraham Lincoln issued the Emancipation Proclamation. The Emancipation Proclamation declared that slaves living in the southern or Confederate states were free. Many slaves joined the Union army. In 1865, the Civil War ended and the southern slaves kept their right to be free. The Emancipation Proclamation led to the 13th Amendment to the Constitution, which ended slavery in all of the United States.

Question 77

What did Susan B. Anthony do?

Answer 77

- **fought for women's rights**
- **fought for civil rights**

Susan B. Anthony was born in Massachusetts on February 15, 1820. She is known for campaigning for the right of women to vote. She spoke out publicly against slavery and for equal treatment of women in the workplace. In 1920, the 19th Amendment to the Constitution gave women the right to vote. Susan B. Anthony died 14 years before the adoption of the 19th Amendment, but it was still widely known as the Susan B. Anthony Amendment. In 1979, she became the first woman whose image appeared on a circulating U.S. coin. The coin is called the Susan B. Anthony dollar and is worth one dollar.

1800s

181

RECENT
AMERICAN
HISTORY

Question 78

Name one war fought by the United States in the 1900s.

Answer 78

- **World War I**
- **World War II**
- **Korean War**
- **Vietnam War**
- **(Persian) Gulf War**

The United States fought five wars in the 1900s: World War I, World War II, the Korean War, the Vietnam War, and the (Persian) Gulf War.

World War I began in 1914. It was a long and bloody struggle. The United States entered the war in 1917 after German submarines attacked British and U.S. ships, and the Germans contacted Mexico about starting a war against the United States. The war ended in 1918 when the Allied Powers (led by Britain, France, Italy, and the United States) defeated the Central Powers (led by Germany, Austria-Hungary, and the Ottoman Empire). The Treaty of Versailles officially ended the war in 1919. World War I was called "the war to end all wars."

World War II began in 1939 when Germany invaded Poland. France and Great Britain then declared war on Germany.

Germany had alliances with Italy and Japan, and together they formed the Axis powers. The United States entered World War II in 1941, after the Japanese attacked Pearl Harbor, Hawaii. The United States joined France, Great Britain, and the Soviet Union as the Allied powers and led the 1944 invasion of France known as D-Day. The liberation of Europe from German power was completed by May 1945. World War II did not end until Japan surrendered in September 1945.

The Korean War began in 1950 when the North Korean Army moved across the 38th parallel into South Korea. The 38th parallel was a boundary established after World War II. This boundary separated the northern area of Korea, which was under communist influence, from the southern area of Korea, which was allied with the United States. At the time, the United States was providing support to establish a democratic South Korean government. The United States provided military support to stop the advance of the North Korean Army. In the Korean conflict, democratic governments directly confronted communist governments. The fighting ended in 1953, with the establishment of the countries of North Korea and South Korea.

From 1959 to 1975, United States Armed Forces and the South Vietnamese Army fought against the North Vietnamese in the Vietnam War. The United States supported the democratic government in the south of the country to help it resist pressure from the communist north. The war ended in 1975 with the fall of Saigon, the capital of South Vietnam. In 1976, Vietnam was under total communist control. Almost 60,000 American men and women in the military died or were missing as a result of the Vietnam War.

On August 2, 1990, the Persian Gulf War began when Iraq invaded Kuwait. This invasion put the Iraqi Army closer to Saudi Arabia and its oil reserves, which supplied much of the world with oil. The United States and many other countries wanted to drive the Iraqi Army out of Kuwait and prevent it from invading other nearby countries. In January 1991, the United States led an international coalition of forces authorized by the United Nations into battle against the Iraqi Army. Within a month, the coalition had driven the Iraqis from Kuwait. The coalition declared a cease-fire on February 28, 1991.

Question 79

Who was president during World War I?

Answer 79

- **(Woodrow) Wilson**

Woodrow Wilson was the 28th president of the United States. President Wilson served two terms from 1913 to 1921. During his first term, he was able to keep the United States out of World War I. By 1917, Wilson knew this was no longer possible, and he asked Congress to declare war on Germany. On January 8, 1918, he made a speech to Congress outlining "Fourteen Points" that justified the war and called for a plan to maintain peace after the war. President Wilson said, "We entered this war because violations of right had occurred which touched us to the quick and made the life of our own people impossible unless they were corrected and the world secure once for all against their recurrence." The war ended that year and Wilson traveled to Paris to work out the details of the surrender by Germany.

Question 80

Who was president during the Great Depression and World War II?

Answer 80

• (Franklin) Roosevelt

Franklin Delano Roosevelt (FDR) was president of the
United States from 1933 until 1945. He was elected
during the Great Depression, which was a period of
economic crisis after the stock market crash of 1929.
His program for handling the crisis was called "the
New Deal." It included programs to create jobs and
provided benefits and financial security for workers
across the country. Under his leadership, the Social
Security Administration (SSA) was established in 1935.
Roosevelt led the nation into World War II after Japan's
attack on Pearl Harbor in December 1941. He gave the
country a sense of hope and strength during a time of
great struggle. Roosevelt was elected to office four times.
He died in 1945, early in his fourth term as president.
His wife, Eleanor Roosevelt, was a human rights leader
throughout her lifetime.

Question 81

Who did the United States fight in World War II?

Answer 81

- **Japan, Germany, and Italy**

The Japanese bombed U.S. naval bases in a surprise attack on Pearl Harbor, Hawaii, on December 7, 1941. The next day, President Franklin D. Roosevelt, as commander in chief of the military, obtained an official declaration of war from Congress. Japan's partners in the Axis, Italy and Germany, then declared war on the United States. The Allies fought against the German Nazis, the Italian Fascists, and Japan's military empire. This was truly a world war, with battles fought in Europe, Africa, Asia, and the Pacific Ocean.

Question 82

Before he was president, Eisenhower was a general. What war was he in?

Answer 82

• World War II

Before becoming the 34th president of the United States in 1953, Dwight D. Eisenhower served as a major general in World War II. As commander of U.S. forces and supreme commander of the Allies in Europe, he led the successful D-Day invasion of Normandy, France, on June 6, 1944. In 1952, he retired from active service in the military. He was elected president of the United States later that year. As president, he established the interstate highway system and in 1953, the Department of Health, Education, and Welfare (now known as Health and Human Services) was created. He oversaw the end of the Korean War. Eisenhower left the White House in 1961, after serving two terms as president.

Question 83

During the Cold War, what was the main concern of the United States?

Answer 83

• Communism

The main concern of the United States during the Cold War was the spread of communism. The Soviet Union (Union of Soviet Socialist Republics, or USSR) was a powerful nation that operated under the principles of communism. The United States and its allies believed that a democratic government and a capitalist economy were the best ways to preserve individual rights and freedoms. The United States and its allies feared the expansion of communism to countries outside the Soviet Union. The Cold War began shortly after the end of World War II and lasted for more than 40 years. It ended with the fall of the Berlin Wall in 1989, the reunification of East and West Germany in 1990, and the breakup of the USSR in 1991.

Question 84

What movement tried to end racial discrimination?

Answer 84

• **civil rights (movement)**

The modern civil rights movement in the United States began in 1954 when the Supreme Court ruled that racial segregation in public schools was unconstitutional. The goal of the civil rights movement was to end racial discrimination against African Americans and to gain full and equal rights for Americans of all races. Using nonviolent strategies such as bus boycotts, sit-ins, and marches, people came together to demand social change. As a result, Congress passed the Civil Rights Act of 1964 and the Voting Rights Act of 1965. The Civil Rights Act made segregation in public facilities and racial discrimination in employment and education illegal. The law protects African Americans, women, and others from discrimination. The Voting Rights Act banned literacy tests and other special requirements that had been used to stop African Americans from registering to vote.

Question 85

What did Martin Luther King, Jr. do?

Answer 85

- **fought for civil rights**
- **worked for equality for all Americans**

Martin Luther King, Jr. was a Baptist minister and civil
rights leader. He worked hard to make America a more
fair, tolerant, and equal nation. He was the main leader of
the civil rights movement of the 1950s and 1960s. Because
of this movement, civil rights laws were passed to protect
voting rights and end racial segregation. King believed in
the ideals of the Declaration of Independence—that every
citizen deserves America's promise of equality and justice.
In 1963, King delivered his famous "I Have a Dream"
speech, which imagines an America in which people of
all races exist together equally. He was only 35 years old
when he received the Nobel Peace Prize in 1964 for his
civil rights work. King was killed on April 4, 1968.

What major event happened on September 11, 2001, in the United States?

Answer 86

- **terrorists attacked the U.S.**

On September 11, 2001, four airplanes flying out of U.S. airports were taken over by terrorists from the Al-Qaeda network of Islamic extremists. Two of the planes crashed into the World Trade Center's Twin Towers in New York City, destroying both buildings. One of the planes crashed into the Pentagon in Arlington, Virginia. The fourth plane, originally aimed at Washington, D.C., crashed in a field in Pennsylvania. Almost 3,000 people died in these attacks, most of them civilians. This was the worst attack on American soil in the history of the nation.

Question 87

Name one American Indian tribe in the United States.

Answer 87

- Cherokee
- Navajo
- Sioux
- Chippewa
- Choctaw
- Pueblo
- Apache
- Iroquois
- Creek
- Blackfeet
- Seminole
- Cheyenne
- Arawak
- Shawnee
- Mohegan
- Huron
- Oneida
- Lakota
- Crow
- Teton
- Hopi
- Inuit

American Indians lived in North America for thousands of years before the European settlers arrived. Today there are more than 500 federally recognized tribes in the United States. Each tribe has its own social and political system. American Indian cultures are different from one tribe to another, with different languages, beliefs, stories, music, and traditional foods. Earlier in their history, some tribes settled in villages and farmed the land for food. Other tribes moved frequently as they hunted and gathered food and resources. The federal government signed treaties with American Indian tribes to move the tribes to reservations. These reservations are recognized as domestic, dependent nations.

Integrated Civics

An understanding of America's geography, symbols, and holidays is important. They provide background and more meaning to historical events and other landmark moments in U.S. history. The following section offers short lessons on our country's geography, national symbols, and national holidays. The geography of the United States is unusual because of the size of the country and the fact that it is bordered by two oceans that create natural boundaries to the east and west. Through visual symbols such as our flag and the Statue of Liberty, the values and history of the United States are often expressed. Finally, you will also learn about our national holidays and why we celebrate them. Most of our holidays honor people who have contributed to our history and to the development of our nation. By learning this information, you will develop a deeper understanding of the United States and its geographical boundaries, principles, and freedoms.

INTEGRATED CIVICS

207

GEOGRAPHY

Question 88

Name one of the two longest rivers in the United States.

Answer 88

- **Missouri (River)**
- **Mississippi (River)**

The Mississippi River is one of America's longest rivers. It runs through ten U.S. states. The Mississippi River was used by American Indians for trade, food, and water before Europeans came to America. It is nicknamed the "Father of Waters." Today, the Mississippi River is a major shipping route and a source of drinking water for millions of people. The Missouri River is also one of the longest rivers in the United States. The Missouri River is actually longer than the Mississippi River. It starts in Montana and flows into the Mississippi River. In 1673, the French explorers Jolliet and Marquette were the first Europeans to find the Missouri River. It is nicknamed "Big Muddy" because of its high silt content.

Question 89

What ocean is on the West Coast of the United States?

Answer 89

- **Pacific (Ocean)**

The Pacific Ocean is on the West Coast of the United States. It is the largest ocean on Earth and covers one-third of the Earth's surface. The Pacific Ocean is important to the U.S. economy because of its many natural resources such as fish. Europeans first learned about the Pacific Ocean in the 16th century. Spanish explorer Vasco Núñez de Balboa reached the ocean in 1514 when he crossed the Isthmus of Panama. Later, Ferdinand Magellan sailed across the Pacific as he traveled around the Earth in search of spices. "Pacific" means "peaceful." Magellan named the Pacific Ocean the "peaceful sea," because there were no storms on his trip from Spain to the spice world. The U.S. states that border the Pacific Ocean are Alaska, Washington, Oregon, California, and Hawaii.

Question 90

What ocean is on the East Coast of the United States?

Answer 90

- **Atlantic (Ocean)**

The Atlantic Ocean is on the East Coast of the United States. The ocean was named after the giant Atlas from Greek mythology. It is the second largest ocean in the world. The Atlantic Ocean is a major sea route for ships. It is one of the most frequently traveled oceans in the world. The Atlantic Ocean is also a source of many natural resources. The Atlantic Ocean was formed by the separation of the North American and European continents millions of years ago. The ocean covers about one-fifth of the Earth's surface. In the middle of the ocean is the Mid-Atlantic Ridge, an immense underwater mountain range that extends the length of the Atlantic and is a source of volcanic activity. The U.S. states that border the Atlantic Ocean are Connecticut, Delaware, Florida, Georgia, Maine, Maryland, Massachusetts, New Hampshire, New Jersey, New York, North Carolina, Rhode Island, South Carolina, and Virginia.

Question 91

Name one U.S. territory.

Answer 91

- **Puerto Rico**
- **U.S. Virgin Islands**
- **American Samoa**
- **Northern Mariana Islands**
- **Guam**

There are five major U.S. territories: American Samoa, Guam, the Northern Mariana Islands, Puerto Rico, and the U.S. Virgin Islands. A U.S. territory is a partially self-governing piece of land under the authority of the U.S. government. U.S. territories are not states, but they do have representation in Congress. Each territory is allowed to send a delegate to the House of Representatives. The people who live in American Samoa are considered U.S. nationals; the people in the other four territories are U.S. citizens. Citizens of the territories can vote in primary elections for president, but they cannot vote in the general elections for president.

Question 92

Name one state that borders Canada.

Answer 92

- Maine
- New Hampshire
- Vermont
- New York
- Pennsylvania
- Ohio
- Michigan
- Minnesota
- North Dakota
- Montana
- Idaho
- Washington
- Alaska

The northern border of the United States stretches more than 5,000 miles from Maine in the East to Alaska in the West. There are 13 states on the border with Canada. The Treaty of Paris of 1783 established the official boundary between Canada and the United States after the Revolutionary War. Since that time, there have been land disputes, but they have been resolved through treaties. The International Boundary Commission, which is headed by two commissioners, one American and one Canadian, is responsible for maintaining the boundary.

Question 93

Name one state that borders Mexico.

Answer 93

- **California**
- **Arizona**
- **New Mexico**
- **Texas**

The border between the United States and Mexico is about 1,900 miles long and spans four U.S. states—Arizona, California, New Mexico, and Texas. The United States established the border with Mexico after the Mexican-American War and the Gadsden Purchase in 1853. The Gadsden Purchase helped the United States get the land it needed to expand the southern railroad. The United States bought this land for $10 million. The land bought through the Gadsden Purchase is now part of the states of Arizona and New Mexico. The U.S. border with Mexico is one of the busiest international borders in the world.

Question 94

What is the capital of the United States?

Answer 94

- **Washington, D.C.**

When the Constitution established our nation in 1789, the capital of the United States was in New York City. Congress soon began discussing the location of a permanent capital city. In Congress, representatives of northern states argued with representatives of southern states. Each side wanted the capital to be in its own region. As part of the Compromise of 1790, the capital would be located in the South. In return, the North did not have to pay the debt it owed from the Revolutionary War. George Washington chose a location for the capital along the Potomac River between Maryland and Virginia. As part of the compromise, Philadelphia, Pennsylvania, became the temporary new location for the capital. In 1800, after ten years, the capital was moved to its current location of Washington, D.C.

Question 95

Where is the Statue of Liberty?

Answer 95

- **New York (Harbor)**
- **Liberty Island [Also acceptable are New Jersey, near New York City, and on the Hudson (River).]**

The Statue of Liberty is on Liberty Island, a 12-acre island in the New York harbor. France gave the statue to the United States as a gift of friendship. French artist Frederic-Auguste Bartholdi made the statue. It shows a woman escaping the chains of tyranny and holding a torch symbolizing liberty. The Statue of Liberty was dedicated on October 28, 1886, 110 years after the signing of the Declaration of Independence. President Grover Cleveland accepted the gift for the American people. The Statue of Liberty is a well-known symbol of the United States and of freedom and democracy. The Statue of Liberty became a symbol of immigration because it was located next to Ellis Island, which was the first entry point for many immigrants during the great waves of immigration. The Statue of Liberty was the first thing new immigrants saw as they approached New York harbor.

GEOGRAPHY

225

SYMBOLS

Question 96

Why does the flag have 13 stripes?

Answer 96

- **because there were 13 original colonies**
- **because the stripes represent the original colonies**

There are 13 stripes on the flag because there were 13 original colonies. We call the American flag "the Stars and Stripes." For 18 years after the United States became an independent country, the flag had only 13 stripes. In 1794, Kentucky and Vermont joined the United States, and two stripes were added to the flag. In 1818, Congress decided that the number of stripes on the flag should always be 13. This would honor the original states that were colonies of Great Britain before America's independence.

Question 97

Why does the flag have 50 stars?

Answer 97

- **because there is one star for each state**
- **because each star represents a state**
- **because there are 50 states**

Each star on the flag represents a state. This is why the number of stars has changed over the years from 13 to 50. The number of stars reached 50 in 1959, when Hawaii joined the United States as the 50th state. In 1777, the Second Continental Congress passed the first Flag Act, stating, "Resolved, That the flag of the United States be made of thirteen stripes, alternate red and white; that the union be thirteen stars, white in a blue field, representing a new Constellation."

Question 98

What is the name of the national anthem?

Answer 98

• The Star-Spangled Banner

During the War of 1812, British soldiers invaded the United States. On the night of September 13, 1814, British warships bombed Fort McHenry. This fort protected the city of Baltimore, Maryland. An American named Francis Scott Key watched the bombing and thought that the fort would fall. As the sun rose the next morning, Key looked toward the fort. He saw that the flag above the fort was still flying. This let him know that the British had not defeated the Americans. Key immediately wrote the words to a poem he called the "Defence of Fort M'Henry." The words of the poem became "The Star-Spangled Banner." Congress passed a law in 1931 naming "The Star-Spangled Banner" the official national anthem. Here are the words to the first verse of the national anthem:

THE STAR-SPANGLED BANNER

Oh, say, can you see, by the dawn's early light,
What so proudly we hailed at the twilight's last gleaming?
Whose broad stripes and bright stars, thro' the perilous fight;
O'er the ramparts we watched, were so gallantly streaming.
And the rockets red glare, the bombs bursting in air,
Gave proof through the night that our flag was still there.
Oh, say, does that star-spangled banner yet wave
O'er the land of the free and the home of the brave?

HOLIDAYS

Question 99

When do we celebrate Independence Day?

Answer 99

- **July 4**

In the United States, we celebrate Independence Day on July 4 to mark the anniversary of the adoption of the Declaration of Independence. After signing the Declaration of Independence, John Adams wrote to his wife, "I am apt to believe that it will be celebrated, by succeeding Generations, as the great anniversary Festival." The Declaration of Independence, written by Thomas Jefferson, explained why the colonies had decided to separate from Great Britain. Americans celebrate the Fourth of July as the birthday of America, with parades, fireworks, patriotic songs, and readings of the Declaration of Independence.

Question 100

Name two national U.S. holidays.

Answer 100

- **New Year's Day**
- **Martin Luther King, Jr. Day**
- **Presidents' Day**
- **Memorial Day**
- **Independence Day**
- **Labor Day**
- **Columbus Day**
- **Veterans Day**
- **Thanksgiving**
- **Christmas**

Many Americans celebrate national or federal holidays. These holidays often honor people or events in our American heritage. These holidays are "national" in a legal sense only for federal institutions and in the District of Columbia. Typically, federal offices are closed on these holidays. Each state can decide whether or not to celebrate the holiday. Businesses, schools, and commercial establishments may choose whether or not to close on these days. Since 1971, federal holidays are observed on Mondays except for New Year's Day, Independence Day, Veterans Day, Thanksgiving, and Christmas.

Resources and Further Reading

Web sites
American Heritage
http://www.americanheritage.com/

Library of Congress: American Memory
http://memory.loc.gov/ammem/index.html

U.S. Citizenship and Immigration Services: Study for the Test
http://www.uscis.gov/citizenship/learners/study-test

The White House: Our Government
http://www.whitehouse.gov/our-government

Books

Ellis, Joseph. *Founding Brothers: The Revolutionary Generation* (New York: Knopf, 2000)

Horwitz, Tony. *Confederates in the Attic: Dispatches from an Unfinished Civil War* (New York: Pantheon, 1998)

McCullough, David. *1776* (New York: Simon & Schuster, 2000)

Skolnick, Solomon. *The Great American Citizenship Quiz* (New York: Walker and Company, 2009)

Williams, Juan. *Eyes on the Prize: America's Civil Rights Years, 1954–1965* (New York: Viking Penguin, 1987)

Wood, Gordon. *The Creation of the American Republic, 1776–1787* (Chapel Hill, NC: University of North Carolina Press, 1969)

Zinn, Howard. *A People's History of the United States* (New York: HarperCollins, 1980)

Image credits